How the book is laid out – many of the [insects in this?] book are distinctive in appearance and wi[ll be?] listed below.

Example – Common Blue

Curren[t...] eviden[ce...]

DESCR[IPTION...] descrip[tion...]

WHERE[TO LOOK...] with g[...] & Oxon Wildlife Trust nature reserves.

WHEN TO LOOK *Flight periods are given*

SIMILAR SPECIES *Key differences are described*

DID YOU KNOW? *Extra fact about the species*

NOTE BOX *Shows eggs, caterpillars or other features such as underside*

Butterflies and moths belong to the same Order of insects called Lepidoptera which means scaly (lepido) winged (ptera). They both undergo four dramatic phases during their life-cycle.

Life-cycle of an Orange-tip

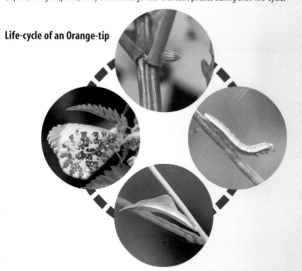

The **butterfly** develops from an egg into a caterpillar, then a chrysalis, and finally an adult butterfly. While there are always exceptions to the general rules, butterflies are usually brightly coloured and active during the day. Their wings are erect and held together at rest and they pupate as an unprotected chrysalis hanging from a branch or other support. The most obvious distinction is their antennae – long shafts with clubbed ends.

The **moth** develops from an egg into a caterpillar and then forms a protective cocoon where it pupates underground or on the ground before emerging as an adult moth. As adults they are usually less bright than butterflies and most are active at night (but in this book only day-flying moths are described). Their wings are held open and folded over their backs while resting. The vast majority of moths have antennae that are either simple filaments, tapering to a point at their ends, or are very complicated 'feathery' structures with many cross filaments.

Butterflies and day-flying moths can be found in a wide variety of habitats: woodland, grassland, heathland, gardens, verges and even waste ground. Some favour the same patch year after year, others travel further afield. The main habitats, and some of the best places to look locally, are mentioned here.

Chalk and limestone grassland

The chalk and limestone grasslands of the Chilterns, Cotswolds and the Downs are home to some of our most attractive species of butterflies and moths. Some of the best sites to visit are – **Berks**: Seven Barrows, Watts Bank and Chawridge Bank nature reserves (all BBOWT sites); **Bucks**: College Lake, Dancersend and Aston Clinton Ragpits nature reserves (all BBOWT sites), Grangelands and Ivinghoe Beacon; **Oxon**: Sydlings Copse, Dry Sandford Pit, Ardley Quarry, Hook Norton Cutting, Hartslock, Chinnor Hill, Oakley Hill and Warburg nature reserves (all BBOWT sites), Aston Rowant National Nature Reserve, Watlington Hill and Aston Upthorpe Down. **LOOK FOR Butterflies**: Small Skipper, Essex Skipper, Silver-spotted Skipper, Dingy Skipper, Grizzled Skipper, Brimstone, Green Hairstreak, Small Copper, Small Blue, Brown Argus, Common Blue, Chalkhill Blue, Adonis Blue, Duke of Burgundy, Painted Lady, Peacock, Dark Green Fritillary, Marsh Fritillary, Marbled White; **Day-flying moths**: Small Purple and Gold, Common Purple and Gold, Straw-barred Pearl, Six-spot Burnet, Narrow-bordered Five-spot Burnet, Cistus Forester, Six-belted Clearwing, Grass Rivulet, Hummingbird Hawk-moth, Dusky Sallow, Silver Y.

Heathland and acid grassland

Heathland, a rare habitat in our three counties, is home to some rare butterflies and day-flying moths as well as more common species. Berkshire holds the vast majority of this special habitat in our area. **Berks**: Wildmoor Heath, Inkpen Common, Decoy Heath and Greenham Common (all BBOWT sites). **LOOK FOR Butterflies**: Essex Skipper, Dingy Skipper, Small Copper, Silver-studded Blue, Common Blue, Grayling, Small Heath; **Day-flying moths**: Straw-barred Pearl, Latticed Heath, Speckled Yellow, Common Heath, Yellow Belle, Grass Wave, Beautiful Yellow Underwing, Dusky Sallow, Silver Y.

Meadows and verges

Although flower-rich meadows are now a rare site in lowland Britain, there are still a good number of sites in our three counties, especially along the Upper Thames and River Ray floodplains. These are home to some of our more familiar butterflies and to several pretty day-flying moths– **Berks**: Inkpen Crocus Field nature reserve; **Bucks**: Bernwood Meadows, Pilch Field and the Upper Ray nature reserves (all BBOWT sites); **Oxon**: Asham Meads, Woodsides Meadow, Chimney Meadows, Oxey Mead and Iffley Meadows nature reserves (all BBOWT sites). **LOOK FOR Butterflies**: Small Skipper, Essex Skipper, Large Skipper, Dingy Skipper, Clouded Yellow, Brimstone, Large White, Small White, Green-veined White, Orange-tip, Brown Hairstreak, Black Hairstreak, Common Blue, Holly Blue, Red Admiral, Painted Lady, Small Tortoiseshell, Peacock, Marbled White, Gatekeeper, Meadow Brown, Small Heath; **Day-flying moths**: Brown China-mark, Six-spot Burnet, Narrow-bordered Five-spot Burnet, Forester, Grass Rivulet, Chimney Sweeper, Common Heath, Scarlet Tiger, Cinnabar, Mother Shipton, Burnet Companion, Silver Y.

Woodland

Some of our most spectacular butterflies and some of the most secretive can be be found in our woodlands. Woodland sites to visit are – **Berks**: Bowdown Woods and Moor Copse nature reserves (BBOWT sites); **Bucks**: Rushbeds Wood, Finemere Wood, Whitecross Green Wood, Little Linford Wood, Homefield Wood and Dancersend nature reserves (all BBOWT sites) and Bernwood Forest; **Oxon**: Foxholes, Sydlings Copse and Warburg nature reserves. **LOOK FOR Butterflies**: Large Skipper, Grizzled Skipper, Wood White, Brimstone, Green-veined White, Purple Hairstreak, White-letter Hairstreak, Black Hairstreak, White Admiral, Purple Emperor, Comma, Silver-washed Fritillary, Speckled Wood, Gatekeeper, Ringlet; **Day-flying moths**: Green Longhorn, Nettle-tap, Speckled Yellow.

Gardens

Gardens can be a haven for some of our most colourful butterflies. One of the best ways to attract butterflies to your patch is by planting nectar-rich flowers. The following plants are particularly popular: lilac buddleia, ice plant, ivy, knapweeds, marjoram and verbena. **LOOK FOR Butterflies**: Brimstone, Large White, Small White, Orange-tip, Holly Blue, Red Admiral, Painted Lady, Small Tortoiseshell, Peacock, Comma; **Day-flying moths**: Small Purple and Gold, Scarlet Tiger, Hummingbird Hawk-moth, Silver Y.

4

Small Skipper
Thymelicus sylvestris

Note: brown-tipped antennae

DESCRIPTION Wingspan: 27–34mm. A small, golden butterfly with an active, buzzing flight. Lively males have the ability to weave slowly then zip sideways and hover in mid-air. Typically rests with forewings pointing upwards in a V, while the hindwings are held parallel to the ground. Antennae brown-tipped.

WHERE TO LOOK A common and widespread species, favouring tall, rough grassland. Seen skipping amongst grassheads in meadows and even gardens; feeds on a variety of flowers including clovers, common bird's-foot-trefoil, knapweeds, thistles and brambles.

WHEN TO LOOK Mid-June–August, peaking in July.

5

Essex Skipper
Thymelicus liineola

Note: black-tipped antennae

DESCRIPTION Wingspan: 26–30mm. Very similar in appearance and behaviour to the Small Skipper but the undersides of their antennae are glossy black rather than brown. Also has an active, buzzing flight and seeks out knapweed and thistle flowers on which to feed.

WHERE TO LOOK Chalk grassland, grassy banks, woodland rides and roadside verges. Large numbers may be seen on good sites, such as Decoy Heath nature reserve in Berks, basking in the late afternoon sunshine before settling to roost amongst the grass.

WHEN TO LOOK Mid-June–August, peaking July, one week later than Small Skipper.

6

Silver-spotted Skipper
Hesperia comma

DESCRIPTION Wingspan: 29–37mm. This handsome skipper is similar in appearance to the Large Skipper but has silver spots on the underside of its hindwings. It has a fast, buzzing flight and can be seen zipping between chalk grassland flowers and frequently basking on patches of bare ground.

WHERE TO LOOK Thin-soiled, south-facing chalk downland with short turf grass and bare ground. The sun-baked, sheltered areas of chalk grassland in the Chilterns provide the ideal conditions. Go to Aston Rowant National Nature Reserve and Watlington Hill (Oxon). This species is rare in Britain and needs warmer conditions than any other British butterfly.

WHEN TO LOOK Late July–August, peaking end August.

> **DID YOU KNOW?**
> Adult Silver-spotted Skippers do not fly in overcast weather or when it is less than 20°C.

Large Skipper
Ochlodes venatus

DESCRIPTION Wingspan: 29–36mm. Unlike the clear golden wings of other skippers, this species has obvious darker mottling on its wings. Males have a distinctive black sex-brand on each forewing and can be seen patrolling for most of the day or perching on sunlit 'launching pads' ready to intercept females or challenge rivals.

WHERE TO LOOK Common and widespread in the three counties but tends to prefer damper and more wooded places than other skippers. Head to sunny areas of rough grassland and open woodland, hedge banks, sheltered roadside verges and gardens, where cock's-foot grows in abundance, as well as bramble and thistle flowers.

WHEN TO LOOK Mid-May–August, peaking mid-June, flying throughout July.

> **DID YOU KNOW?**
> The Large Skipper was once known as 'The Chequered Hog' or 'Streakt Cloudy' by early butterfly collectors.

8

Dingy Skipper
Erynnis tages

DESCRIPTION Wingspan: 27–34mm. This species can be difficult to identify because it is extremely fast, darting over short grass before zooming up into the sky. More than any of its relatives the grey-brown Dingy Skipper resembles a moth, roosting with its wings folded around a flower or grasshead.

WHERE TO LOOK South-facing downland, heathland, meadows and old quarries. The Dingy Skipper breeds and flies on the same site each year, favouring sheltered sites such those found at Hartslock and Oakley Hill nature reserves in Oxon and Watt's Bank reserve in Berks. There it basks in warm sunshine on bare ground for long periods of time.

WHEN TO LOOK Mid-April–mid-June.

DID YOU KNOW?

One of the UK's most rapidly declining species, but increasing in number on carefully managed BBOWT sites.

Grizzled Skipper
Pyrgus malvae

DESCRIPTION Wingspan: 23–29mm. This small, attractive skipper has dark grey-brown upperwings with conspicuous white spots. Males are known for their ferocious dog-fights and rivals try to outmanoeuvre one another by circling, diving and soaring in the air. Always alert, this butterfly is best seen basking in sunlit places.

WHERE TO LOOK Now rare outside central-southern England, the declining Grizzled Skipper can be found on a hot day in the sunny woodlands of the Chilterns and on Greenham Common in Berks. The following BBOWT nature reserves are also worth a visit: Bernwood Meadows, Dancersend and Whitecross Green Wood (Bucks), Ardley Quarry, Oakley Hill and Warburg Nature Reserve (Oxon), Watt's Bank and Chawridge Bank (Berks).

WHEN TO LOOK April–June, peaking in May.

DID YOU KNOW?

The larval foodplant of Grizzled Skipper is wild strawberry.

Wood White
Leptidea sinapis

DESCRIPTION Wingspan: 35–40mm. This small and dainty butterfly is the rarest of all British whites and declining in the UK. The delicacy of its wings, their rounded shape, the long, slender body and a slow, flapping flight all help to distinguish the Wood White from its relatives.

WHERE TO LOOK Though Wood Whites were once found at Whitecross Green Wood in Oxon, only two populations in the three counties now remain, on the border with Northants. Wood Whites favour sheltered, sunlit woodland rides with bugle, ragged-robin and greater bird's-foot-trefoil. In hot, dry weather males can be seen drinking from the edges of muddy puddles, a behaviour known as 'puddling', to absorb mineral salts.

WHEN TO LOOK Late April–June, peaking in May.

Clouded Yellow
Colias crocea

DESCRIPTION Wingspan: 52–58mm. A fast-flying and active summer migrant from the Mediterranean. Upperwings are a rich egg-yolk yellow in males and dark-bordered yellow in females (pictured below). 'Clouded Yellow years' often occur with large immigrations of red admirals and painted ladies.

WHERE TO LOOK In a good year the Clouded Yellow can turn up anywhere. Usually seen in ones or twos across the three counties, but major immigrations can bring in vast numbers from southern Europe and north Africa, depending on weather-pattern fluctuations. This is the only species of butterfly in the UK to be able to breed on modern fertilised grasslands which often feature sown clover.

WHEN TO LOOK February–October.

SIMILAR SPECIES

Pale Clouded Yellow *Colias hyale* (52–62mm) and **Berger's Clouded Yellow *Colias alfacariensis*** (50–60mm), both very rare immigrants.

Brimstone
Gonepteryx rhamni

DESCRIPTION Wingspan: 60–74mm. The male brimstone is highly conspicuous and often considered to be the herald of spring. The female is much paler and can be confused with a large white on the wing. The underwings of the male provide perfect camouflage as they look exactly like yellow-green leaves.

WHERE TO LOOK Common and widespread, wherever buckthorn and alder buckthorn, the larval foodplants grow. The brimstone can be seen almost every month of the year – it is our longest-lived species. Look along hedgerows, around woods and gardens where you can find purple flowers including wild teasel, purple-loosestrife and thistles.

WHEN TO LOOK First warm days of spring, second brood: high summer.

> **DID YOU KNOW?**
> The old English name for the brimstone, the 'butter-coloured fly' is said to have given rise to the word 'butterfly'.

Large White
Pieris brassicae

DESCRIPTION Wingspan: 53–70mm. The Large White is a handsome butterfly with a strong and powerful flight. The underwings are yellowish and the upperwings are a creamy-white with black tips. The female (pictured left) has two spots on the forewing. The upright, yellow eggs are laid in clusters on either side of a brassica leaf.

WHERE TO LOOK The Large White is common and widespread in the three counties and is considered a pest by gardeners due to their voracious caterpillars that devour brassica crops. They can also be seen in meadows, downs, waste ground, farms and allotments as well as in gardens.

WHEN TO LOOK May–November.

Note: yellow eggs in clusters

14

Small White
Pieris rapae

DESCRIPTION Wingspan: 45–57mm. The Small White is smaller and less striking than its close relative, the Large White. The male usually has a black spot in the centre of each forewing. White eggs are laid singly on brassica leaves or nasturtiums, changing to yellow then grey. Similar to the Large White it hibernates as a chrysalis.

WHERE TO LOOK The Small White is one of our most common butterflies and can be seen almost anywhere, especially gardens with flowers and vegetables, though they favour white or pale blossoms.

WHEN TO LOOK April, peaking in mid-May. Second brood: July–October.

Note: eggs laid singly

15

Green-veined White
Pieris napi

DESCRIPTION Wingspan: 40–52mm. A pretty white, much more delicate than the 'cabbage whites' with a fluttering flight pattern. Its underwings are particularly attractive with a series of veins, decorated by scales that appear as green stripes. These markings can vary greatly but females are more heavily striped than males. First brood males and females are significantly smaller than their offspring.

WHERE TO LOOK Green-veined White is fairly common in the three counties and can be seen in damp, sheltered grassland and along woodland rides.

WHEN TO LOOK April–May. Second brood: July–September.

DID YOU KNOW?

The male Green-veined White showers the female with 'love dust' so strong that even humans can detect its scent which is similar to lemon verbena.

Orange-tip
Anthocharis cardamines

DESCRIPTION Wingspan: 40–52mm. The vibrant male Orange-tip is a sure sign that spring has arrived. Males spend much of their time wandering through the countryside searching for a mate. Females are much more secretive, hiding in scrub for most of the day. When at rest these butterflies have the perfect camouflage, with mottled moss-green underwings.

WHERE TO LOOK Meadows, woodland, hedgerows, sheltered lanes, ditches and gardens, wherever there is cuckooflower, the butterfly's main foodplant. Good BBOWT sites to visit include Bernwood Meadows (Bucks), Asham Meads, Iffley Meadows and Chimney Meadows (Oxon), Moor Copse and Inkpen Crocus Field (Berks).

WHEN TO LOOK Mid-April–June.

DID YOU KNOW?

The male's bright orange colouring acts as a warning to potential predators that they are bitter to taste and best avoided.

Green Hairstreak
Callophrys rubi

DESCRIPTION Wingspan: 27–34mm. The Green Hairstreak is an entertaining butterfly to watch and will launch itself from a vantage point to fend off encroaching males by engaging in sustained aerial battles. The butterfly with the most stamina wins the day, only to find that its favourite perch has been taken by another. The green underside of the hindwing often has a line of white dots but these can be absent.

WHERE TO LOOK Hawthorn bushes in full sunshine, such as those on the heathland at Greenham Common (Berks) and the chalk downland at Aston Clinton Ragpits, College Lake and Dancersend (Bucks), Hartslock and Warburg Nature Reserve (Oxon), all BBOWT sites. Males will perch for an hour at a time waiting for passing females.

WHEN TO LOOK Mid-April–late June, peaking mid-May–mid-June.

DID YOU KNOW?

The Green Hairstreak is the only British butterfly to have truly green wings.

18

Brown Hairstreak
Thecla betulae

Note: sculptured white eggs

DESCRIPTION Wingspan: 36–45mm. The largest of our five native hairstreak butterflies is elusive. Brown Hairstreaks seldom fly when the temperature drops below 20°C and males spend much of their lives in the treetops. The female is brighter than the male. They often settle with wings open, revealing large, colourful orange patches. The white and beautifully intricate, bun-shaped eggs are much more visible and can be found on dark blackthorn twigs between November and April.

WHERE TO LOOK Blackthorn hedges along the Bucks/Oxon border are a stronghold for this scarce butterfly. Head to Bernwood Forest as well as BBOWT nature reserves: Bernwood Meadows, Whitecross Green Wood, Asham Meads and Upper Ray Meadows.

WHEN TO LOOK Late July–early September.

Purple Hairstreak
Favonius quercus

DESCRIPTION Wingspan: 31–40mm. The Purple Hairstreak is a woodland butterfly and basks on sunny boughs, unlike most of its relatives, with their wings open. Towards evening males launch themselves at passing females and challenge rivals above the treetops. The sparkle of their wings in the sunlight is considered to be one of the highlights of the butterfly season.

WHERE TO LOOK Sheltered oak and ash woodland with sunny clearings beneath which many ant nests can be found. Ideal places include Rushbeds Wood and Little Linford Wood (Bucks), as well as Warburg Nature Reserve and Sydlings Copse (Oxon), all BBOWT sites.

WHEN TO LOOK Early July–September, peaking end July.

DID YOU KNOW?

It is the only British hairstreak to have an eye-spot on the underside, next to the short tail.

White-letter Hairstreak
Satyrium w-album

DESCRIPTION Wingspan: 25–35mm. You will need binoculars to glimpse this lively little hairstreak, spinning in the sunshine around the treetops. When it settles it always closes its wings revealing distinctive white markings on the undersides which resemble the letter 'W' sideways-on. White-letter Hairstreaks feed on the flowers of creeping thistle.

WHERE TO LOOK Head for the warm, sunny elm hedgerows bordering woodland sites such as Finemere Wood and Homefield Wood in Bucks and Woodsides Meadow in Oxon, all BBOWT sites.

WHEN TO LOOK Late June–mid-July.

DID YOU KNOW?

In the 1970s Dutch elm disease led to the loss of many elm trees and with them many colonies of the White-letter Hairstreak.

21

Black Hairstreak
Satyrium pruni

DESCRIPTION Wingspan: 34–40mm. This butterfly is a great rarity and enthusiasts will travel the breadth of the country to see it. Warm brown in colour, it has a series of black spots along the inner edge of the orange-red band on its hindwings, unlike the White-letter hairstreak which has a black one. It feeds on the flowers of wild privet and dog-rose.

WHERE TO LOOK South-facing blackthorn hedgerows specifically managed for the Black Hairstreak by BBOWT including those at Bernwood Meadows, Finemere Wood, Rushbeds Wood, Whitecross Green Wood and Upper Ray Meadows in Bucks. Bernwood Forest (Forestry Commission).

WHEN TO LOOK Mid-June–July.

DID YOU KNOW?

The Black Hairstreak was one of the last butterflies to be discovered locally in 1918, in Bernwood Forest by a schoolboy, W. F. Burrows.

Small Copper
Lycaena phlaeas

DESCRIPTION Wingspan: 26–36mm. An exquisite and lively little lowland butterfly with bright copper-coloured forewings. Fast flying and always on the move even rotating its body while supping nectar from flowers. Males are feisty and always ready to launch themselves at any passing insect. Small Coppers roost head-down in tall grass.

WHERE TO LOOK Well-drained warm banks, heaths, chalk downland, old quarries and patches of rough waste ground, as well as country gardens. Local BBOWT nature reserves include Bernwood Meadows (Bucks), Asham Meads, Dry Sandford Pit, Glyme Valley (Oxon), Bowdown Woods and Greenham Common (Berks).

WHEN TO LOOK May, second brood: July–August, third brood: September–October.

DID YOU KNOW?

The hairy caterpillar is well camouflaged for its life on common sorrel and sheep's sorrel leaves.

Small Blue
Cupido minimus

DESCRIPTION Wingspan: 18–27mm. The Small Blue is our smallest and daintiest butterfly. Both males and females have smoky grey-blue upperwings and appear bluer in flight. When at rest the undersides of their rounded wings are clear silver-blue, patterned with delicate black dots with no trace of orange.

WHERE TO LOOK The Small Blue favours thin-soiled habitats including sunlit embankments, old quarries, railway lines and road verges. They can be seen at College Lake in Bucks and Seven Barrows and Watt's Bank in Berks, all BBOWT sites. Though widespread, this butterfly is declining. The caterpillars feed on the flowers of kidney vetch and the eggs are laid singly in the flower-heads of the same plant.

WHEN TO LOOK Mid-May–June. Second brood: high summer.

DID YOU KNOW?

The caterpillars of the Small Blue can 'sing' as loudly as those of the Adonis Blue.

24

Silver-studded Blue
Plebejus argus

DESCRIPTION Wingspan: 28–32mm. The Silver-studded Blue gets its name from the light blue reflective studs on the underside of the wings of most adults. Adults rarely fly a few centimetres above the ground with a slow, fluttering flight. Females lay their eggs near nests of black ants and gorse, ling and other heathers. This butterfly has a fascinating relationship with black ants: the ants provide protection to the caterpillar and they feed on honeydew secreted by the caterpillar.

WHERE TO LOOK The rare Silver-studded Blue has declined enormously across the UK and is a Priority Species. It is confined to small colonies on heathland with sparse vegetation. An expanding colony can be found at Wildmoor Heath nature reserve in Berks, thanks to BBOWT's careful management with periodic grazing, cutting blocks of heather and clearing birch.

WHEN TO LOOK Late June onwards, peaking mid-July lasting into August.

Brown Argus
Aricia agestis

DESCRIPTION Wingspan: 25–31mm. A small, lively butterfly with chocolate-brown upperwings and orange bands which are bolder on the females than the males. It is similar in appearance to the female Common Blue, but is smaller with no blue coloration. Like the Common Blue, it will roost communally on grass stems.

WHERE TO LOOK The Brown Argus is restricted to small, localised colonies, usually on chalk grassland, but more recently along woodland rides and sheltered fields. Look for the flowers of common rock-rose and the crane's-bill family in Bernwood Forest (Forestry Commission), Seven Barrows and Watt's Bank (Berks), Homefield Wood (Bucks), Ardley Quarry and Hartslock (Oxon) all BBOWT sites.

WHEN TO LOOK Mid-May–late June. Second brood: July–September.

DID YOU KNOW?

Males gather at the base of a slope where they perch or patrol in search of passing females.

Common Blue
Polyommatus icarus

Note: undersides of mating pair

DESCRIPTION Wingspan: 29–36mm. The male Common Blue is vivid lilac blue in contrast to the more subtle, blue-brown female (pictured below). Both have a spot on the forewing near the body and orange marks on the edges of the hindwings. This butterfly has a short, fast flight as it flits from one flower to the next.

WHERE TO LOOK Our most common and widely distributed blue butterfly readily seen on heathlands, grassland, banks and roadside verges. It is a regular visitor to flower-filled gardens. The best time to look is early morning and late afternoon.

WHEN TO LOOK Mid-May–mid-June. Second brood: late July–September.

Chalkhill Blue
Lysandra coridon

Note: underside

DESCRIPTION Wingspan: 33–40mm. Males and females are completely different in appearance (dimorphic). Males are a beautiful milky blue whereas females are a deep brown. They are most often seen in bright sunshine, when males appear stunning sky blue. They gather together at night to roost in tall tussocks of grass.

WHERE TO LOOK Now more scarce than it once was, head to herb-rich chalk downland with flowers such as scabious and knapweed. The best local sites include Aston Clinton Ragpits (Bucks), Hartlock (Oxon), Seven Barrows and Watt's Bank (Berks), nature reserves managed by BBOWT.

WHEN TO LOOK Mid-July–August.

Adonis Blue
Lysandra bellargus

DESCRIPTION Wingspan: 30–40mm. Males have dazzling sky blue wings, while females are brown. Both have characteristic black lines that cross the white edges on the wings. As a caterpillar and chrysalis, this butterfly is protected by ants that feed on the honeydew it secretes.

WHERE TO LOOK A scarce sun-loving species found on warm, south-facing slopes of chalk grassland with short grazed turf containing horseshoe vetch, the foodplant of both caterpillars and adults. Numbers have declined drastically across the UK due to loss of grasslands. To catch a glimpse of this beautiful butterfly head to Hartslock nature reserve in Oxon.

WHEN TO LOOK Mid-May–June. Second brood: August–September.

DID YOU KNOW?

Named after Adonis, the Greek god of beauty and desire – this butterfly was once highly prized and collected.

Holly Blue
Celastrina argiolus

Note: ichneumon wasp egglaying

DESCRIPTION Wingspan: 26–34mm. The Holly Blue is easier to identify at rest. It has bright blue wings with pale blue undersides marked with small black spots. Females have black edges to their wings. They only open their wings fully in weak sunshine.

WHERE TO LOOK Best seen in early spring as it emerges earlier than other blue butterflies and unlike its close relatives, flies around trees and bushes, rather than grassland. It favours shrubs including holly (spring) and ivy (late summer) in gardens, parks and open countryside. Every few years numbers of the Holly Blue drop dramatically when its caterpillars are killed by the grubs of a parasitic ichneumon wasp.

WHEN TO LOOK Mid-April–June. Second brood: late July–August.

Duke of Burgundy
Hamearis lucina

DESCRIPTION Wingspan: 29–34mm. This tiny, orange and brown springtime butterfly has distinctive chequered patterning on its wings and is the only European member of the tropical 'metalmark' family. Males are more active than females. With the decline in coppicing, this butterfly is nearing extinction in many parts of the country.

WHERE TO LOOK This is one of the most rapidly declining butterflies in Britain, and a Priority Species for conservation organisations. Head to the scrubby grassland and sunny woodland clearings with primrose and cowslips on Ivinghoe Beacon in Bucks for the possibility of a sighting. A small colony of the Duke of Burgundy did exist at Dancersend nature reserve in Bucks, though no recent sightings have been recorded by BBOWT or the local branch of Butterfly Conservation.

WHEN TO LOOK Late April or early May–early June.

White Admiral
Limenitis camilla

DESCRIPTION Wingspan: 56–66mm. This beautiful black butterfly with white banded wings is a favourite among many butterfly enthusiasts. It is a truly elegant creature, gliding down from the tops of trees to the woodland floor and up again in a few effortless wing beats. The patterning of the underwings is particularly attractive.

WHERE TO LOOK An elusive butterfly normally seen in ones or twos along sunny woodland edges and rides with patches of bramble. They spend much of their time basking in the oak canopy and drinking aphid honeydew from the leaves. Locations with regular sightings include: Bowdown Woods (Berks), Finemere Wood, Rushbeds Wood and Whitecross Green Wood (Bucks), Warburg Nature Reserve and Foxholes (Oxon), all BBOWT.

WHEN TO LOOK Mid-June, peaking in 2nd–3rd week of July.

DID YOU KNOW?
Females lay their eggs on the leaves of wild honeysuckle.

Purple Emperor
Apatura iris

Note: female lacks purple sheen

DESCRIPTION Wingspan: 70–92mm. The magnificent male Purple Emperor, known affectionately as 'His Majesty', has the purple sheen to its upperside and a distinctive yellow proboscis. Both the male and the larger female have beautiful undersides with a striking eye-spot to scare off predators.

WHERE TO LOOK High up in the oak canopy where it feeds on aphid honeydew. Males descend to the ground occasionally to feed on salts, found in mud and animal droppings. If you are lucky you might spot this scarce and elusive butterfly in Finemere Wood, Rushbeds Wood, Whitecross Green Wood and Bernwood Forest in Bucks.

WHEN TO LOOK June-August, best seen early morning or late afternoon.

33

Red Admiral
Vanessa atalanta

DESCRIPTION Wingspan: 64–78mm. The strong-flying Red Admiral is a familiar migrant visitor, arriving from North Africa and continental Europe in the summer months remaining until late autumn. It is easy to identify with its velvety black wings, red bands and white blotches. Its undersides are mottled and dark providing excellent camouflage.

WHERE TO LOOK Common and widespread in the three counties and a regular visitor to gardens. Red Admirals feed on the nectar of buddleia and ivy flowers and the sugars produced by fermenting fruit. Females lay their eggs in patches of common nettles.

WHEN TO LOOK March–November.

DID YOU KNOW?

You can attract Red Admirals to your garden by planting buddleia and ivy and leaving windfall apples and plums on the ground to rot.

34

Painted Lady
Vanessa cardui

DESCRIPTION Wingspan: 58–74mm. The distinctive Painted Lady has orange-brown wings with black and white spots. It is a fast-flying butterfly, arriving from North Africa, the Middle East and central Asia in late summer to feed on thistles in gardens and other flower-filled sites.

WHERE TO LOOK A common and widespread migrant that can be found in any warm, dry open places including meadows, downland, heath, waste ground and gardens. In a 'Painted Lady year' large numbers swarm upwards through Europe into Britain.

WHEN TO LOOK March–October, peaking July–September, depending on a good year.

> **DID YOU KNOW?**
> The cosmopolitan Painted Lady inhabits every continent except Australia and Antarctica.

Small Tortoiseshell
Aglais urticae

DESCRIPTION Wingspan: 45–62mm. The upperwings of Small Tortoiseshells have warm orange and yellow tones with bold black markings. Their smoky-brown undersides offer the perfect camouflage, giving the appearance of old, dried leaves, allowing them to hibernate in wood piles, hollow trees, garden sheds and garages undisturbed.

WHERE TO LOOK A common and familiar garden and wayside butterfly, wherever there are large patches of nettles. Worryingly this butterfly has suffered a decline in recent years.

WHEN TO LOOK Late March–October. Two broods per year.

> **DID YOU KNOW?**
> Hot summers result in more brightly coloured Small Tortoiseshells, the cooler the weather, the duskier the butterfly.

Peacock
Aglais io

DESCRIPTION Wingspan: 63–75mm. The glamorous Peacock has evolved three clever defence mechanisms: dramatic eye-spots on its wings to confuse predators, camouflaged undersides resembling dried leaves and the ability to 'hiss' by rubbing its wings. The female lays eggs on common nettle and a mass of black caterpillars live and feed together under their web of silk.

WHERE TO LOOK This species is widespread and found almost anywhere, including open, sunny woodlands and flower-rich gardens.

WHEN TO LOOK March–September.

Note: caterpillars on nettle

Comma
Polygonia c-album

Note: 'bird dropping' caterpillar

DESCRIPTION Wingspan: 50–64mm. The vivid orange and brown Comma is a master of disguise throughout its life-cycle. The caterpillar resembles a bird dropping, the chrysalis, a withered leaf, and the ragged profile and marbled-brown undersides of the adult butterfly make it the leaf mimic *par excellence* during hibernation. This butterfly gets its name from the white comma-shaped mark on its brown undersides.

WHERE TO LOOK Woodland clearings and sunny rides with catkins in spring and bramble flowers in summer. The following BBOWT sites provide the ideal conditions: Finemere Wood (Bucks), Foxholes, Oakley Hill and Sydlings Copse (Oxon).

WHEN TO LOOK March–late October, peaking early April then July–mid-September.

8

Dark Green Fritillary
Argynnis aglaja

DESCRIPTION Wingspan: 56–68mm. This fast and powerful flier can be difficult to watch so it's best to find a patch of thistles or knapweed and wait for the butterfly to come to you. Males are more active than females spending much of their time on the wing. Females lay eggs close to violets, the larval foodplant.

WHERE TO LOOK Early morning and late afternoon one or two butterflies may be seen flitting from flower to flower on open, windswept grassland habitats such as those at Gomm Valley in Bucks and Warren Bank in Oxon, both BBOWT sites.

WHEN TO LOOK Mid–early September, peaking early July.

> **DID YOU KNOW?**
>
> This butterfly gets its name from the green tint on the underside of its hindwings.

Silver-washed Fritillary
Argynnis paphia

Note: female is larger and duller

DESCRIPTION Wingspan: 69–80mm. This large fritillary is both beautiful and graceful with a gliding flight. It has distinctive pointed wings with silver streaks on the undersides. The male is a vibrant tangerine-orange with four black sex brands along the forewings. The female is duller in colour but larger with larger black spots, though fewer 'stripes'.

WHERE TO LOOK Swooping through dappled woodland glades, particularly oak woods, and along sunny rides settling on bramble flowers. Dancersend, Finemere Wood, Rushbeds Wood (Bucks), Warburg Nature Reserve (Oxon) and Bowdown Woods (Berks) all provide the ideal habitat.

WHEN TO LOOK Mid-June–August, peaking first week of August.

Marsh Fritillary
Eurodryas aurinia

DESCRIPTION Wingspan: 30–50mm. The chequered wings of the Marsh fritillary are more brightly coloured than any of its relatives and bring to mind panels of stained-glass. Males are much smaller than females. This butterfly only flies in sunshine.

WHERE TO LOOK The Marsh Fritillary is one of our most rapidly declining species because of the significant loss of suitable wetland habitat. They breed in the same patch of damp, tussocky grassland each year. There is only one residual tiny population left in the three counties, at Seven Barrows nature reserve in Berks. Once widespread, this threatened and nationally rare butterfly is a UK Priority Species for conservation organisations.

WHEN TO LOOK May–early July.

> **DID YOU KNOW?**
> The caterpillars of the Marsh Fritillary bask together on their web to retain warmth.

Speckled Wood
Pararge aegeria

DESCRIPTION Wingspan: 46–56mm. A velvety brown butterfly with obvious creamy white patches on the wings. On cool spring days males will perch in full sunshine on the ground or on low vegetation along woodland rides. In warmer temperatures they will patrol through the tree canopy searching for females on the wing.

WHERE TO LOOK Widespread in semi-shaded woodland, hedgerows and gardens with damp areas of long grass. Head to any of BBOWT's woodland nature reserves in the three counties.

WHEN TO LOOK Any time from late February–November. Two to three broods per year.

> **DID YOU KNOW?**
> The Speckled Wood has the unique ability to overwinter as a caterpillar or chrysalis.

Wall
Lasiommata megera

DESCRIPTION Wingspan: 45–53mm. The name of this eye-catching orange and brown butterfly comes from its habit of basking on walls, stones and bare ground to soak up the sun's warmth. Its pale brown undersides provide effective camouflage against such a background. Females are larger and brighter than males.

WHERE TO LOOK The Wall has declined significantly in many inland areas of central England and is retreating to coastal habitats. It is almost extinct in the three counties with the last sightings recorded by Butterfly Conservation before 2008. It favours dry, unimproved grassland with exposed patches of broken ground.

WHEN TO LOOK Late April–early June. Second brood: August–September.

> **DID YOU KNOW?**
> The first English name for the female was 'the golden marbled butterfly with black eyes', and the male 'the London Eye'.

Marbled White
Melanargia galathea

Note: female underside

DESCRIPTION Wingspan: 50–60mm. This distinctive black and white grassland butterfly is a highlight of any summer's day. Large groups of adults can be seen feeding on the purple flowers of wild marjoram, field scabious, thistles and knapweeds or basking in the sunlight with their wings held open. The bold markings are a warning to predators that the butterfly is poisonous.

WHERE TO LOOK Widespread in grassland, woodland clearings, roadside verges and railway embankments such as Bernwood Meadows, College Lake, Dancersend (Bucks), Chimney Meadows, Chinnor Hill, Dry Sandford Pit, Sydlings Copse and Warburg Nature Reserve (Oxon).

WHEN TO LOOK Mid-June–August.

Grayling
Hipparchia semele

DESCRIPTION Wingspan: 51–62mm. At rest with its wings closed the Grayling is difficult to spot due to its highly effective silver-grey camouflage. However, when disturbed the forewing reveals a vivid eye-spot to ward off potential predators and enemies. In flight this butterfly appears much larger – it is in fact our largest brown butterfly.

WHERE TO LOOK The Grayling is a nationally declining butterfly and a high conservation priority. It is a heathland rarity in the three counties and found in Berks at Greenham Common, Bowdown Woods and Decoy Heath nature reserves.

WHEN TO LOOK Early July–mid-September, peaking end of July.

> **DID YOU KNOW?**
>
> During courtship the male Grayling bows to the female with its wings apart, and draws her antennae over his scent glands.

Gatekeeper
Prionia tithonus

DESCRIPTION Wingspan: 37–48mm. Orange and brown with a black eye-spot on the wing with two white pupils, in contrast to the Meadow Brown that has one pupil. This butterfly gets its name from where it is often seen, in groups of flowers by gateways, along field margins and hedgerows. It is often accompanied by Meadow Brown and Ringlet butterflies.

WHERE TO LOOK Common and widespread along sheltered, sunny hedgerows and on woodland rides, wherever there is tall, wild grass.

WHEN TO LOOK Early July, peaking first week in August.

> **SIMILAR SPECIES**
>
> The **Meadow Brown** (p.47) is larger and has a black eye-spot with just one white pupil instead of the Gatekeeper's two white pupils.

Meadow Brown
Maniola jurtina

DESCRIPTION Wingspan: 40–60mm. The Meadow Brown is the most common
butterfly in Britain and can be seen in large numbers in overcast weather and even
light rain. It is regularly mistaken for the Gatekeeper and the Ringlet, but the black
eye-spot has just one white pupil.

WHERE TO LOOK Plentiful and widespread on any patch of wild grassland, in hay
meadows, roadside verges, hedgerows and woodland rides.
Males can be seen darting through tall grasses
looking for females. Creeping thistle is a
favourite foodplant.

WHEN TO LOOK June–September, peaking
late July.

DID YOU KNOW?

The female is more brightly
coloured than the male. The male
has hardly any orange coloration
on the upperwings.

Small Heath
Coenonympha pamphilus

DESCRIPTION Wingspan: 33–37mm. Paler and smaller than other browns, the Small
Heath flies in sunshine and always keeps its wings closed when at rest. When
wings are held upwards a bright eye-spot is displayed in a pale brown triangle,
which is used to deflect attacks from predators.

WHERE TO LOOK Flying close to the ground in a jerky flight pattern on well-drained
grassland and downland, heathland and woodland rides. Many
colonies have disappeared in recent decades and it
is a Priority Species for conservation. To find
this butterfly go to Greenham Common in
Berks, Ardley Quarry, Dry Sandford Pit
and Warburg Nature Reserve in Oxon.

WHEN TO LOOK Mid-May, peaking
mid-June. Second brood:
early August–mid-September.

DID YOU KNOW?

The early English name for this
butterfly was 'Golden Heath Eye'.

Ringlet
Aphantopus hyperantus

DESCRIPTION Wingspan: 42–52mm. A dark velvety-brown butterfly with distinctive ringed circles on the underwings which give the butterfly its name. The circles can vary in number and size. The female is paler than the male. Both male and female have conspicuous white fringes on their wings.

WHERE TO LOOK Amongst tall, lush tussocks of damp grass in semi-shade along woodland rides, glades, verges and riverbanks, where bramble and wild privet flowers can be found. Active even in cloudy weather. Dancersend (Bucks), Asham Meads, Foxholes, Sydlings Copse, Warburg Nature Reserve (Oxon) and Greenham Common and Moor Copse (Berks).

WHEN TO LOOK Late June–mid-August.

> **DID YOU KNOW?**
>
> In France the Ringlet is known as 'The Sorrowful', in Germany 'Brown Wood-Bird'.

Green Longhorn
Adela reaumurella

DESCRIPTION Wingspan: 14–18mm. This micro-moth has metallic dark-green forewings and paler hindwings. All moths in the longhorn family are true to their name with long, slender antennae. The male Green Longhorn has white antennae that are longer than the female's. When at rest it has a pointed, tent-like appearance. The caterpillar grows on the ground in leaf litter, beneath oak and birch.

WHERE TO LOOK The Green Longhorn flies in the sunshine in the woodlands of Bowdown Woods (Berks) and Sydlings Copse (Oxon). Males can be seen dancing around sunlit areas in the dozens, settling on leaves or sometimes swarming around treetops.

WHEN TO LOOK Mid-April–June.

> **SIMILAR SPECIES**
>
> **Early Longhorn** *Adela cuprella* (14–16mm) flies April–May and **Brassy Longhorn** *Nemophora metallica* (16–20mm) flies June–August. Both have shorter antennae.

50

Nettle-tap
Anthophila fabriciana

DESCRIPTION Wingspan: 10–15mm. This tiny, mottled brown micro-moth has pale markings with two white bars on the edge of each forewing. The caterpillars are pale brown with dark brown spots. They live in webs on the top of leaves that they curl upwards.

WHERE TO LOOK Commonly seen and heard buzzing in swarms around patches of common (stinging) nettles in open woodland, hedgerows, waste ground, gardens. Head to Dry Sandford Pit and Sydlings Copse (Oxon).

WHEN TO LOOK April–November. There are at least two broods.

> **DID YOU KNOW?**
> The Nettle-tap holds its wings open when at rest.

Brown China-mark
Elophila nymphaeata

DESCRIPTION Wingspan: 25–33mm. The Brown China-mark gets its name from the markings on its wings which resemble the identification marks that Chinese porcelain producers put on their pots. The patterning can vary, ranging from pale to dark patches and streaks.

WHERE TO LOOK A fairly common species of moth, whose caterpillar develops underwater, feeding on water plants. On a summer evening head for the vegetation growing by the fringes of ponds, lakes, slow-moving rivers and canals. These moths are easily disturbed. A good place to look is in the grassland by the pond at Bowdown Woods in Berks.

WHEN TO LOOK May–September.

> **SIMILAR SPECIES**
> The **Beautiful China-mark** *Nymphula nitidulata* (20–25mm) is white and silver. Its larvae favour water-lilies at places such as Hinksey Fields, along Hinksey stream in Oxford.

Small Purple and Gold
Pyrausta aurata

DESCRIPTION Wingspan: 15–18mm. This pretty day-flying micro-moth has regal purple forewings with gold markings. The dark hindwings are striped with a thick, golden bar. As the pink-tinged caterpillars develop they spin leaves together with silken thread to form a protective covering.

WHERE TO LOOK A common species found feeding on wild marjoram flowers on the chalk grasslands of the Chilterns, such as Warburg Nature Reserve (Oxon). It can also be seen in old quarries, gardens (where it can be common), and open woodland. It is also known by gardeners as the 'mint moth' because its foodplant is also mint.

WHEN TO LOOK March–September. Two broods per year.

> **SIMILAR SPECIES**
>
> The **Common Purple and Gold** *Pyrausta purpuralis* (15–22mm) is a much brighter purple but lacks the gold markings on the hindwings.

Straw-barred Pearl
Pyrausta despicata

DESCRIPTION Wingspan: 14–19mm. The wings of the Straw-barred Pearl are grey-brown with pale brown markings that can vary. It ranges from very grey to rich brown and even the markings can appear yellower. This somewhat plain-looking micro-moth is a member of the 'pyralid' family with characteristically long, narrow forewings and broader hindwings.

WHERE TO LOOK Active in bright sunshine and as dusk falls on chalk and limestone habitats. The large expanse of grassland at Greenham Common in Berks is a good place to look.

WHEN TO LOOK Mid-April–June. Second brood: July–September.

> **SIMILAR SPECIES**
>
> Faded specimens of the **Common Purple and Gold** can look similar in appearance.

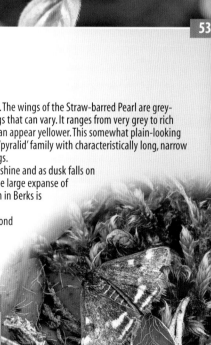

54

Six-spot Burnet
Zygaena filipendulae

DESCRIPTION Wingspan: 25–40mm. This is the only burnet moth with six red spots on each forewing, though the number of spots can vary and may be fused in some instances. In bright light the greenish-black wings have a metallic sheen. The Six-spot Burnet has a slow, buzzing flight.

WHERE TO LOOK Widespread on grasslands, downland, woodland rides and roadside verges. The Six-spot Burnet can be seen flying in sunshine displaying similar behaviour to a butterfly by flitting from one flower to another, such as thistles, knapweed and scabious. Mating pairs are a frequent sight. Head to BBOWT reserves including Dancersend (Bucks), Hartslock and Sydlings Copse (Oxon).

WHEN TO LOOK June–August.

DID YOU KNOW?

Its bright colours warn potential predators that it is poisonous.

Narrow-bordered Five-spot Burnet
Zygaena lonicerae

DESCRIPTION Wingspan: 30–46mm. This burnet is similar in appearance to the Five-spot Burnet but has longer forewings and more pointed hindwings. Eggs are laid on the leaves of bird's-foot-trefoil. The yellow-green caterpillars with black markings feed on meadow vetchling and clovers. Their light-coloured, papery cocoons are easy to spot high up on a plant stem.

WHERE TO LOOK Often seen in the same locations as the Six-spot Burnet moth such as chalk downland, rough grassland and woodlands. All burnets live in colonies and can be numerous where clovers, trefoils and vetches grow.

WHEN TO LOOK Late June–August.

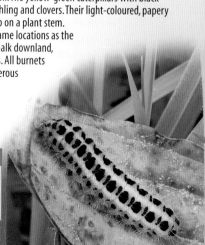

SIMILAR SPECIES

Six-spot Burnet (see above) and the more uncommon **Five-spot Burnet** *Zygaena trifolii* (32–40mm).

Forester
Adscita statices

DESCRIPTION Wingspan: 24–29mm. Like most members of the burnet group, this day-flying moth takes to the wing in sunshine and its metallic green coloration makes it very easy to identify. The Forester's name is thought to derive from its colour – the Lincoln Green of Robin Hood and Sherwood Forest.

WHERE TO LOOK The Forester is the most commonly occurring of the three forester species. Despite its name it is not a woodland species but a grassland moth, favouring chalk downland and damp neutral grassland. Look for devil's-bit scabious, field scabious and marsh thistle, flowers preferred by the Forester, at sites such as Rushbeds Wood and Bernwood Meadows (Bucks).

WHEN TO LOOK Mid-May–July.

SIMILAR SPECIES

The **Cistus Forester *Adscita geryon*** (20–25mm) prefers chalk grassland where rock-rose grows.

Six-belted Clearwing
Bembecia ichneumoniformis

DESCRIPTION Wingspan: 17–22mm. This distinctive species might be mistaken for a hornet or wasp at first glance. It is however, one of 15 species of clearwing moths. Unlike a wasp or hornet it has four wings rather than two, a smaller head than other insects, narrow wings that have a cross-bar and long, slender antennae.

WHERE TO LOOK Chalk and limestone grassland where caterpillars develop deep in the roots of kidney vetch and bird's-foot-trefoil. Head to Dry Sandford Pit nature reserve in Oxon.

WHEN TO LOOK Late June–mid-August.

SIMILAR SPECIES

The **Currant Clearwing *Synanthedon tipuliformis*** (18–22mm) has three yellow bands on its lower abdomen and can be seen flying around currant bushes towards the end of June.

58

Grass Rivulet
Perizoma albulata

DESCRIPTION Wingspan: 20–26mm. The Grass Rivulet is a small, chalky-white moth patterned with grey and brown lines running across the forewings. The caterpillar's foodplant are the ripening seeds of yellow rattle.

WHERE TO LOOK Usually flies from late afternoon to early dusk, but also by night, and is often found near yellow rattle on grassland habitats, particularly on chalk and limestone. Sometimes large numbers can be seen flying together.
Search for this moth in the large area of limestone grassland at Sydlings Copse nature reserve in Oxon.

WHEN TO LOOK May–early July.

SIMILAR SPECIES

Pale creamy-yellow forms of the **Yellow Shell *Camptogramma bilineata*** (28–32mm) are similar in appearance but have many more fine bands and will fly in the day if disturbed.

Chimney Sweeper
Odezia atrata

DESCRIPTION Wingspan: 27–30mm. A sooty-black moth, fading to brownish-black, with white fringes around the tips of the upperwings. Sometimes large numbers of Chimney Sweepers can be seen together perching on the tall stems of grass. The caterpillars eat the leaves of the pignut plant.

WHERE TO LOOK Flying rapidly in bright sunshine over grassland and along hedgerows, usually in damp meadows such as Pilch Field (Bucks), Oxey Mead, Yarnton Mead and Glyme Valley in Oxon. Males will sometimes fly in overcast weather.

WHEN TO LOOK June–August.

DID YOU KNOW?

Chimney Sweepers remain in the egg stage from the end of summer until the middle of the following spring.

Latticed Heath
Chiasmia clathrata

DESCRIPTION Wingspan: 22–32mm. A small, yellowish moth with striking patterning on the wings that resembles a net or lattice. Coloration and markings can be variable ranging from yellowish to much paler. While most moths fold their wings down along their bodies when at rest, the Latticed Heath basks with its wings open and settles with them held aloft, like a butterfly.

WHERE TO LOOK Open grassland, heathland and waste ground, open woodland and gardens.

WHEN TO LOOK May–June. Second brood: August–September.

SIMILAR SPECIES

Common Heath (p.63) , though this species rests with wings held downwards. The **Grizzled Skipper** (p.9) also looks similar.

Speckled Yellow
Pseudopanthera macularia

DESCRIPTION Wingspan: 28–30mm. This easily recognised moth is small, warm yellow in colour and speckled with brown blotches. Towards the end of August the green caterpillars work their way down to the ground before pupating in dead leaves. Throughout the winter the chrysalis will remain in the leaf litter before emerging as an adult the following spring.

WHERE TO LOOK The open, sunlit woodland at Bowdown Woods and the scrubby grassland at Greenham Common, both sites with plentiful wood sage. Eggs are laid on wood sage, white dead-nettles, yellow archangel and hedge woundwort.

WHEN TO LOOK Mid-May–June.

SIMILAR SPECIES

Yellow Shell *Camptogramma bilineata* (28–32mm) varies in colour from pale creamy yellow to orange-yellow but with darker and lighter shaded bands. It is often disturbed by day.

Common Heath
Ematurga atomaria

DESCRIPTION Wingspan: 22–34mm. This small moth can range in colour from white to grey or brown. Both the forewing and hindwing have dark bands running across them, sometimes fuzzy or speckled. The male has particularly feathery antennae which helps to tell it apart from similar moths and butterflies. The female is much whiter than the male.

WHERE TO LOOK Common and widespread, flying by day, especially in warm weather most often on heathland, but also open woodland, meadows and roadside verges. On heathland its caterpillars feed on heathers, elsewhere they feed on clovers, trefoils and vetches. Head to the Berkshire heathlands or Sydlings Copse and Oxey Mead in Oxon, both BBOWT sites.

WHEN TO LOOK May–August.

SIMILAR SPECIES

Latticed Heath (p.61), **Dingy Skipper** (p.9) and **Grizzled Skipper** (p.9).

Yellow Belle
Aspilates ochrearia

DESCRIPTION Wingspan: 28–36mm. A pale yellow medium-sized moth with two brown stripes across the forewing. Females are usually less yellow than males and do not have feathery antennae. The caterpillars feed on a wide range of foodplants including wild carrot and plantain.

WHERE TO LOOK Locally common at Greenham Common in Berks but it is more of a coastal species. Look in the low vegetation and grass where the Yellow Belle is easily disturbed from rest during the day. It flies in hot sunshine and from dusk into the night.

WHEN TO LOOK May–June. August–September.

SIMILAR SPECIES

The **Grass Wave** *Aspilates gilvaria* (36–41mm), also found on Berkshire heaths, is paler yellow and has one forewing stripe. The males have feathery antennae.

Scarlet Tiger
Callimorpha dominula

DESCRIPTION Wingspan: 52–58mm. This large and very colourful moth has a dipping and rising flight pattern. The forewing is shiny black with white and yellow blotches. The hindwings are mostly red – used to flash a warning at potential predators. The black and hairy caterpillars with white and yellow spots feed on many plants including common comfrey.

WHERE TO LOOK On a sunny day in late afternoon or early evening on marshy grassland, fenland, damp meadows and riverbanks, such as Dry Sandford Pit, Lashforn Lane Fen, Parsonage Moor (Oxon) and Moor Copse (Berks), all BBOWT reserves.

WHEN TO LOOK June–July.

Note: caterpillar on comfrey

Cinnabar
Tyria jacobaeae

Note: caterpillars on ragwort

DESCRIPTION Wingspan: 35–45mm. The medium-sized Cinnabar has glossy red and black wings and a weak, fluttering flight. Both the caterpillars and the moths have striking colours which serve as warnings to birds and other predators that they are inedible. It is one of the most poisonous moths in Britain.

WHERE TO LOOK Common in the three counties. Cinnabars fly in the sunshine and can be seen in long grass where they are readily disturbed from rest. Looking for the stripy caterpillars on ragwort is one of the easiest ways to spot the moth. Greenham Common in Berks is a good site to visit.

WHEN TO LOOK May–August, sometimes lasting into October.

Mother Shipton
Euclidia mi

DID YOU KNOW

Flies with the similar **Burnet Companion** (see below) and the **Dingy Skipper** butterfly (p.9).

DESCRIPTION Wingspan: 30–34mm. This medium-sized brown moth gets its name from the pattern on the wings said to resemble the profile of a Yorkshire witch, Mother Shipton, who lived in the 16th century. The caterpillars eat clovers, common bird's-foot-trefoil, black medick, lucerne and grasses.

WHERE TO LOOK The Mother Shipton is a characteristic grassland species. It can be seen in flower-rich grasslands such as Bernwood Meadows and Upper Ray Meadows on the Bucks/Oxon border, as well as Woodsides Meadow (Oxon) and in the small meadow at Bowdown Woods (Berks), flying rapidly for short bursts then resting and feeding on flowers.

WHEN TO LOOK May–early July.

67

Burnet Companion
Euclidia glyphica

SIMILAR SPECIES

Flies with the similar **Mother Shipton** (see above) and the **Dingy Skipper** butterfly (p.9).

DESCRIPTION Wingspan: 28–34mm. A medium-sized brown moth with marbling on its forewings and orange-yellow hindwings. Very alert and easily disturbed from rest in the long grass. Caterpillars are pale yellow with grey-brown markings and feed at night on clovers, black medick, lucerne and bird's-foot-trefoil.

WHERE TO LOOK A common but localised day-flying moth often in the company of burnet moths which is how it got its name. It flies rapidly in sunshine and warm, overcast weather and rests often, usually sheltering in long grass in hay meadows, on downland, embankments and along woodland rides. Head to Bernwood Meadows and Upper Ray Meadows (Bucks), Sydlings Copse (Oxon) and Decoy Heath in Berks, all BBOWT sites.

WHEN TO LOOK May–July.

Hummingbird Hawk-moth
Macroglossum stellatarum

DESCRIPTION Wingspan: 50–58mm. This hawk-moth is a summer visitor from the south of France and north Africa and can vary in number from one year to the next. It has orange-brown hindwings and grey forewings with a black and white lower body. Once believed to be a messenger of good news.

WHERE TO LOOK Usually seen anywhere, including gardens, as a lone moth hovering in front of flowers, like a hummingbird. It inserts its long tongue deep into the petals of tubular plants such as geraniums, petunias, honeysuckles, periwinkles and verbenas, before rapidly moving to the next flower in a characteristic darting motion.

WHEN TO LOOK In sunshine throughout summer and autumn.

SIMILAR SPECIES

The rarer **Narrow-bordered Bee Hawk-moth** *Hemaris tityus* (41–46mm) and **Broad-bordered Bee Hawk-moth** *Hemaris fuciformis* (46–52mm) both have a similar buzzing flight.

Beautiful Yellow Underwing
Anarta myrtilli

DESCRIPTION Wingspan: 24–28mm. A small, fast-flying moth with boldly patterned red-brown and white forewings and yellow hindwings broadly bordered with black. This moth creates a mosaic of colours as it feeds on the nectar of heathland flowers.

WHERE TO LOOK The Beautiful Yellow Underwing is restricted to heathland habitats in our area but is also found on moorland in other parts of Britain. It can be seen flying rapidly in the sunshine just above vegetation and hovering in front of heather at Decoy Heath nature reserve in Berks. In overcast weather it can be seen at rest on heather and bell heather.

WHEN TO LOOK Late April–August.

Note: green caterpillar on heather

Dusky Sallow
Eremobia ochroleuca

DESCRIPTION Wingspan: 34–37mm. A medium-sized mottled brown and straw coloured moth with a dark broken band across the forewing. The caterpillars are glossy pale green with white markings and feed on grasses including cock's-foot, false oat grass and common couch.

WHERE TO LOOK Widely distributed in the three counties on chalk grassland, heathland, scrub, open woodland and embankments. Usually seen flying in sunshine or feeding on the flowers of knapweed and ragwort. Head to Dry Sandford Pit nature reserve in Oxon.

WHEN TO LOOK July–September.

DID YOU KNOW?

The caterpillars of the Dusky Sallow burrow down just beneath the ground to spin a cocoon and pupate.

Silver Y
Autographa gamma

DESCRIPTION Wingspan: 32–52mm. Both its common and scientific names describe this moth's characteristic feature – the white mark on each forewing that can be read as either 'Y' or as the symbol for the Greek letter gamma.

WHERE TO LOOK This medium-sized silver-grey moth is one of our most commonly seen day-flying moths. As well as visitors to Britain from continental Europe, there is a resident population and the Silver Y can be seen in large numbers in gardens, woodlands and many other places, feeding on flowers. They can also be seen at Hartslock, Sydlings Copse and Warburg Nature Reserve in Oxon and Greenham Common in Berks.

WHEN TO LOOK April–October, most numerous late summer–early autumn.

SIMILAR SPECIES

The **Beautiful Golden Y** ***Autographa pulchrina*** (36–44mm) has golden-orange forewings.

Species index